Table **of Contents**

What is the value of innovation?

Advancements in Technology

Benchmark
EDUCATION

Advancements in Technology

Student Objectives

I will be able to:

- **Read and analyze informational texts about the development of communications technology.**

- **Share ideas with my peers.**

- **Build my vocabulary knowledge.**

- **Write informational, narrative, and opinion texts.**

Credits
Editor: Jeffrey B. Fuerst
Contributing Editors: Brett Kelly, Joanne Tangorra
Creative Director: Laurie Berger
Art Directors: Melody DeJesus, Kathryn DelVecchio-Kempa, Doug McGredy, Chris Moroch
Production: Kosta Triantafillis
Director of Photography: Doug Schneider
Photo Assistant: Jackie Friedman

Photo credits: Cover B: Everett Collection/Newscom; Cover D: © JASON SZENES/epa/Corbis; Table of Contents A, Table of Contents B, Page 19A, 19B, 23: Granger, NYC; Table of Contents C, Page 26: © LUONG THAI LINH/epa/Corbis; Page 2: Underwood Archives; Page 3A: © Tom Grill/Corbis; Page 3B: © Xinhua / Alamy; Page 6: Library of Congress; Page 7, 15: © Bettmann/CORBIS; Page 8A, 8C: Everett Collection/Newscom; Page 8D: © Lake County Museum/CORBIS; Page 9C: © Ted Soqui/Corbis; Page 12: ASSOCIATED PRESS; Page 14: © dmac / Alamy; Page 18: © Pictorial Press Ltd / Alamy; Page 29B: © Underwood & Underwood/Corbis

Printed in Dongguan, China. 8557/0118/14122

ISBN: 978-1-4900-9193-8

Tips for Text Annotation

As you read closely for different purposes, remember to annotate the text. Use the symbols below. Add new symbols in the spaces provided.

Symbol	Purpose
<u>underline</u>	Identify a key detail.
☆	Star an important idea in the margin.
① ② ③	Mark a sequence of events.
(magma)	Circle a key word or phrase.
?	Mark a question you have about information in the text. Write your question in the margin.
!	Indicate an idea in the text you find interesting. Comment on this idea in the margin.

Your annotations might look like this.

Notes	
I like the way Cinderella expresses herself.	2 Next, I ran to add kindling to the fires in their rooms. I would not have heard the end of it if my stepsisters' large, ugly feet touched a cold floor. There was no kindling in either room, so I had to run to the backyard to gather up twigs and sticks. Thorns cut my fingers and briars stuck in my hair.
I wonder why Cinderella puts up with her mean stepsisters?	3 My older stepsister demanded soft-boiled eggs. My younger stepsister yelled for medium-boiled eggs. I flew to the kitchen to make their breakfasts. I toil round the clock.

LEXILE® is a trademark of MetaMetrics, Inc., and is registered in the United States and abroad.

E-book and digital teacher's guide available at benchmarkuniverse.com.

BENCHMARK EDUCATION COMPANY
145 Huguenot Street • New Rochelle, NY • 10801

Toll-Free 1-877-236-2465
www.benchmarkeducation.com
www.benchmarkuniverse.com

Remember to annotate as you read.

Notes

Alexander Graham Bell: "It Talks!"

by Kathy Furgang

1   Telephones have connected people to one another since the late 1800s. Alexander Graham Bell invented this important communication tool. Bell was born in Scotland in 1847. His mother was deaf; this made Bell want to learn all about sound. He learned how it travels as vibrations, or sound waves. He wanted to find new ways for people to communicate.

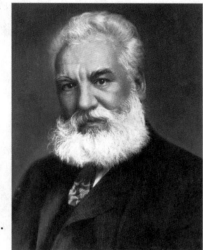
Alexander Graham Bell

2   As an adult, Bell taught at several schools for deaf students in Boston. His wife was also deaf. All the while, he kept learning more about how sound works. He also studied the human voice.

3   Bell dreamed that people would one day "talk with electricity." At the time, people could only send telegraphs. These were coded messages sent over wires using a system of clicks and blips. The messages were then written down and delivered by hand.

4 Bell began to experiment with electric wires. He wanted spoken words to travel a long way from person to person. After many tries, Bell finally succeeded. On March 10, 1876, a call reached his assistant in the next room: "Mr. Watson, come here. I want to see you." These were the famous words of the first phone call ever made. Bell had achieved his goal.

5 Bell brought his telephone to the 1876 World's Fair in Philadelphia, Pennsylvania. He called it an "electrical speech machine." People were amazed at Bell's work. The leader of Brazil, Emperor Pedro II, was at the fair. When he heard sound through the telephone wire, he dropped the phone. "It talks!" he cried out.

6 Bell's invention was revolutionary. In 1877, he established the Bell Telephone Company. Three years later there were more than 130,000 phones in American homes. Bell's invention paved the way for how we communicate today.

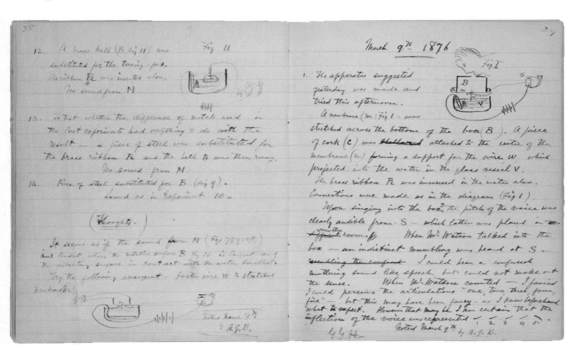

Bell got a patent to protect his invention.

Remember to annotate as you read.

Notes

From Telephone to FaceTime

by Caleb Adams

1   "The day will come when the man at the telephone will be able to see the distant person to whom he is speaking." Alexander Graham Bell spoke these words back in the 1800s. The inventor of the telephone knew what he was talking about. Thanks to technology, people can now talk face-to-face with someone thousands of miles away.

2   When telephones were invented, most people did not understand how electrical machines worked. Therefore, some people were afraid of telephones. Rumors spread that conversations were not private or that telephones could cause people to become deaf. Others did not see why telephones were useful. President Rutherford B. Hayes, nineteenth president of the United States, tested the telephone back in 1876. He had one put into the White House a year later. However, he had this to say about the telephone: "An amazing invention, but who would ever want to use one?"

An Idea Takes Hold

3   Ring! At first, the telephone was a strange new idea to the world. People did not even know what to say when they answered it. Alexander Graham Bell thought "Ahoy," a call used by sailors, worked well. But inventor Thomas Alva Edison had another idea. He hoped the word "Hello" would catch on as the best telephone greeting. He put the greeting "Hello" in his operating manuals for the telephone. By 1880, people were saying "Hello" to start phone conversations.

4   Once people saw how useful a telephone could be, the demand for phones went up sharply. By 1900, Bell's company had almost 600,000 phones in use. That number increased to 6 million by 1910.

5   When telephones were first installed in homes, people could make calls only through an operator's help. By the 1920s, people could call numbers without an operator.

switchboard operators, around 1915

6   The phone became part of people's everyday lives. Push-button telephones replaced rotary-dial phones in 1963. People were reluctant to give up their old phones, so Bell Telephone created a video to demonstrate how easy it was to use push-button phones. Not having to dial also saved time.

Off-the-Wall Technology

7   For almost a century, telephone signals could only be sent along cables and into the walls of buildings. Cable phones are called "landlines." But another important discovery came along in 1973: the world's first cell phone. People could now carry a phone down the street! Cellular phone technology is different from landline technology. Signals go through the air instead of through wires. Signals go from large towers to the phone. But the first cell phones were big and cost a lot of money, too. Not many people had them.

The History of the Telephone

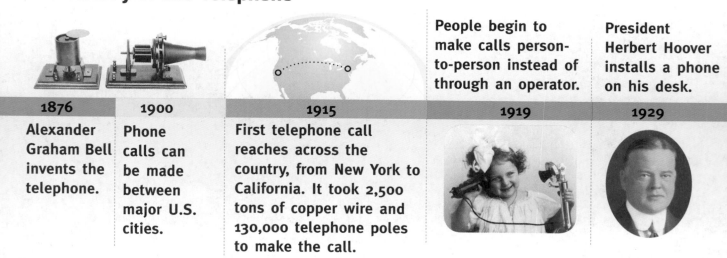

People begin to make calls person-to-person instead of through an operator.

President Herbert Hoover installs a phone on his desk.

1876	1900	1915	1919	1929
Alexander Graham Bell invents the telephone.	Phone calls can be made between major U.S. cities.	First telephone call reaches across the country, from New York to California. It took 2,500 tons of copper wire and 130,000 telephone poles to make the call.		

8   Cell phones did not get small enough to fit into people's pockets until around 2000. Once that happened, more and more people bought them. Many phones became "smarter," too. These "smartphones" can do a lot more than make calls. They work like computers. In 2003, a computer software program called Skype was introduced, allowing people to make video calls on the Internet. Now video calls can be made from a cell phone. People can send photos and written messages with cell phones, too. They can surf the Internet. According to Digital Trends, a technology information website, as of 2014, there were more cell phones than people on Earth.

9   We have come a long way from Alexander Graham Bell's first phone!

1963	1968	1973	2000	2003	2010	2014
For the first time, people can push numbered buttons to make a call instead of using a round, or rotary, dial.	911 becomes the nationwide phone number to call in case of an emergency.		Cell phones are made to be the size of a deck of cards. By this year, there are 100 million cell phone users in the United States.	Computer software application Skype is founded in Sweden by Niklas Zennström and Janus Friis.	Video calling software FaceTime is introduced on the Apple iPhone, a brand of cell phone.	
	EMERGENCY CALL 911	The first portable cell phone call is made in New York City.				There are more cell phones than people on Earth.

Word Study Read

Remember
to annotate
as you read.

Notes

The Longest Wire

1   Before the invention of the telephone (1876), the telegraph (1844) let people communicate across great distances. Wires carried signals over land and across state lines. Communication across the Atlantic Ocean was a different story. Letters took weeks to arrive from overseas. Businessman Cyrus Field imagined a time when a message from North America would reach Europe in just one day! Could one telegraph wire stretch across the whole Atlantic Ocean?

2   Many thought it wasn't possible. Field was sure it was. Inventors made a strong cable that could carry the signals. Marine scientists mapped a route across the ocean floor. Engineers built machines for steamships to carry and lay miles and miles of heavy wire.

3   In 1857, two ships set out to lay the wire. The cable snapped 200 miles from shore. Field tried again in June of 1858. This time, a huge storm nearly sank one of the ships. Plus, the cable broke again. That same summer, Field tried yet again. This time everything worked. Field himself rowed ashore to make the final connection. America and Europe were joined! People celebrated with parties and fireworks.

4   It had taken twelve years for Field's dream to come true. When it did, people could share news across the ocean almost instantly.

BuildReflectWrite

Build Knowledge

Identify patterns in the life of Alexander Graham Bell that influenced his invention of the telephone. Then show how these patterns impacted his work. Cite evidence from both texts.

Alexander Graham Bell	
Pattern 1	**Impact**
Pattern 2	**Impact**

Reflect

What is the value of innovation?

Based on this week's texts, write down new ideas and questions you have about the essential question.

_____

_____

_____

_____

_____

_____

Writing to Sources

Narrative

Pretend you are Alexander Graham Bell. Write two paragraphs in which you describe your meetings with Emperor Pedro II and President Hayes. Make sure your narrative includes facts and details from "Alexander Graham Bell: 'It Talks!'" and "From Telephone to FaceTime."

Notes

Thomas Edison: "It Sings!"

by Elizabeth Michaels

"Genius is one percent inspiration and 99 percent perspiration."

—THOMAS EDISON

1   American inventor Thomas Alva Edison was born on February 11, 1847, in Milan, Ohio. He was the seventh and youngest child in his family. People called him "Al" as a boy, after his middle name. Edison barely spoke a word until he was almost four years old. After that, he started asking many questions about how things worked. One of his most common questions was just one word: "Why?" His parents tried to answer all his questions, but sometimes they simply did not know the answers. It was Edison's curiosity that helped him become a great inventor!

Edison was born in this house in Ohio, in 1847.

A Curious Mind

2   At seven, Edison went to school in a one-room schoolhouse with children of all ages. The teacher thought there was something wrong with Edison because he questioned everything. He also did poorly

Edison grew up very curious about the world.

in mathematics and had speech problems. After three months, Edison's mother removed him from school. She decided to teach him at home. She knew her son was smart and needed more attention.

3   For years, Edison was happy learning at home. He loved reading all kinds of books. By the age of twelve, Edison started asking his parents very hard questions about science. They did not know the answers. Unfortunately, Edison could not return to school because he had severe hearing problems. He was completely deaf in his left ear and 80 percent deaf in his right ear. So he continued to learn on his own. His favorite subject became the new technology of the time—electricity.

Young Inventor

4   As a young teen, Edison tried to earn some money for his family. He handed out fliers, or advertisements, that asked people to vote for Abraham Lincoln as the next American president. He also learned how to send telegraphs. Telegraph messages were sent along electric wires as a series of clicks and blips. These were then translated into a code of dots and dashes. At fifteen, Edison moved to Boston, Massachusetts, to be a telegraph operator. He translated the coded messages that came in to the office.

5   At the same time, Edison continued to work on his own projects. He came up with his first patent, an electric voting machine. The only problem was that his machine did not sell. Edison was disappointed. After that, he decided he would "never waste time inventing things that people would not want to buy."

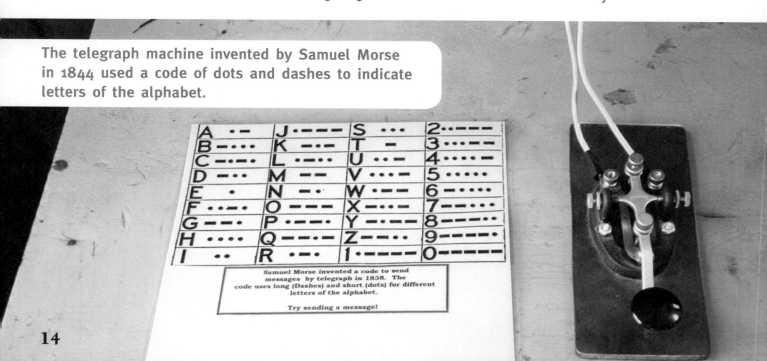

The telegraph machine invented by Samuel Morse in 1844 used a code of dots and dashes to indicate letters of the alphabet.

Edison said about inventing, "I find out what the world needs, then I proceed to invent it."

The Laboratory

6   Edison moved to New York City in 1869. Two years later, he developed the Universal Stock Printer. This machine was a new type of stock "ticker." It sent the most current prices for company stock shares through telegraph wires. A printing device at the other end printed out the prices on a long ribbon of paper. The telegraph company paid Edison $40,000 for his improved machine! It was his first successful invention.

7   With the money from his stock ticker and other inventions, Edison opened a laboratory in Menlo Park, New Jersey. He hired talented scientists to help him develop and test new inventions. "Inspiration can be found in a pile of junk," Edison once said. "Sometimes, you can put it together with a good imagination and invent something."

Great Inventions

8   In 1876, Edison attended the Centennial Exhibition world's fair in Philadelphia, Pennsylvania. He displayed one of his automatic telegraph machines. It could send messages at high speeds. Edison also displayed an electric pen with a tiny motor. It was used to make copies of documents. This invention got a lot of attention at the exhibition and won awards for its innovative design. While at the fair, Edison was inspired by what he saw. His visit sparked many new ideas. Edison was especially curious about a device on display called a "telephone." Invented by Alexander Graham Bell, this device transmitted the sound of the human voice over wires.

9   In 1877, Edison worked on a way to improve Bell's telephone. He made it possible for voices to sound louder and clearer over the telephone wires. "I never pick up an item without thinking of how to improve it," Edison had said. He also made improvements on his telegraph machines.

10   As a result of his experiments, Edison ended up with a new kind of sound machine. He invented the first phonograph. He found a way to record sound on a cylinder coated with tinfoil. The machine had one needle for recording sound. It also had a needle for playing back sounds. As sounds vibrated, the needle pressed into the cylinder in the same pattern.

11   The first words Edison spoke into the machine were from the nursery rhyme "Mary Had a Little Lamb." The machine played his own words back to him.

12   Edison knew this invention was important. He saw the many ways it could help people communicate. People could record letters on the cylinders instead of writing them down on paper. Books could be read onto the cylinders and then played back to blind people. Families could record and keep the sounds of their children's voices. Many of these ideas led to new tools for communication.

The phonograph was only one of Edison's many important inventions.

13   Edison started a company that sold phonographs and cylinders. People bought cylinders with their favorite music on it. Later, wax discs known as "records" became the most used format.

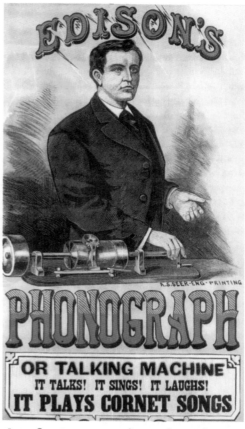

A 7-foot poster introduced Edison's phonograph.

14   Edison's fame increased. In 1878 he was invited to the White House to demonstrate the phonograph to President Rutherford B. Hayes. Edison was nicknamed the "Wizard of Menlo Park" by a newspaper reporter.

15   Even after so many inventions, Edison still brimmed with great ideas. For two years, he and the scientists in his lab worked hard on a new project. They wanted to develop a lightbulb that used less electricity than other bulbs and could burn much longer. Edison's lab tested thousands of ideas and materials. In 1879, they produced a lightbulb that glowed for more than fourteen hours, longer than any other lightbulb. Until that time, typical bulbs lasted only a few minutes.

16   Edison eventually produced bulbs that could glow for over 1,500 hours. They looked very much like the lightbulbs we see in our homes today.

17   By the age of eighty-three, Thomas Edison had obtained 1,093 patents for his inventions. His work improved the way in which we communicate every day. Edison died in 1931. By that time, most American homes had both electric lights and a phonograph machine.

Edison's Most Popular Inventions

Invention	What It Is Used For
stock printer	improved telegraph transmission of stock market information
incandescent lightbulb	artificial light
phonograph	recording and playing back sound
mimeograph	making copies of documents
storage battery	recharging batteries
kinetoscope	early motion picture device for viewing moving pictures
electric pen	making copies of documents
movie camera	recording films
fruit preserver	keeping fruit fresh
electric train track turntable	changing the direction trains travel

Remember to annotate as you read.

Notes

George Eastman and the Kodak Camera

1   In 1878, George Eastman, age twenty-four, worked as a bank clerk in Rochester, New York. He was planning a trip to a Caribbean island. His coworkers suggested that he take pictures.

2   At that time, taking pictures wasn't easy. Cameras were bulky and heavy. Photographers had to spread wet chemicals on glass plates that went inside the camera. Then they placed the camera on a tripod to take the picture. They had to work with more chemicals to make the image appear.

3   Eastman wanted to make the process simpler. He performed experiments in his mother's kitchen. In three years, he invented a dry plate that could be used with cameras.

4   Eastman didn't stop there. He wanted to invent a smaller, portable camera that the general public could use. Over time, he replaced the heavy glass plates with thin, light film. In 1888, his invention was ready. The first Kodak cameras appeared in stores.

5   The Kodak camera became one of the most popular inventions of all time. Workers in Eastman's factories shared in the company's profits. Eastman also donated money to various groups. As one of the "fathers of photography," George Eastman was the very picture of success!

BuildReflectWrite

Build Knowledge

Compare and contrast Alexander Graham Bell and Thomas Edison. Support your ideas with details and examples from the texts.

Alexander Graham Bell	Thomas Edison
Background	Background
Work ethic	Work ethic
Impact	Impact

Reflect

What is the value of innovation?

Based on this week's texts, write down new ideas and questions you have about the essential question.

_____

_____

_____

_____

_____

_____

Writing to Sources

Informative/Explanatory

Drawing on two reading selections from this unit, write a short essay that explains how the telephone was invented and how this new device affected people's lives. Use text evidence from the two reading selections as the basis of your explanation.

Notes

From Phonograph to Playlist

by Ben Foster

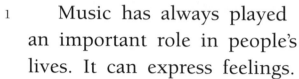

"Music is the universal language of mankind."
—HENRY WADSWORTH LONGFELLOW, POET

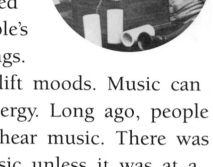

1   Music has always played an important role in people's lives. It can express feelings. It can tell stories. It can lift moods. Music can even give people more energy. Long ago, people had to go to concerts to hear music. There was no other way to hear music unless it was at a live performance.

2   Today's technology helps people play and listen to music anywhere. They can listen to music while driving a car, sitting on a beach, or flying in an airplane. Astronauts play music and even make their own music in space.

3   One invention started the modern music business. It was the phonograph. This amazing invention has led to many others. People can now make music part of their lives anywhere, anytime.

Phonograph

4   The word *phonograph* means "writing sound" in Greek. It is the perfect word to describe how early recordings worked. The early machine recorded sounds with a needle onto a cylinder covered in foil. The machine "wrote" the sounds. The sounds could then be played back again.

5   Thomas Edison developed the phonograph in 1877. It opened up a new world for music lovers. Edison was quite proud of his new invention. He showed it to the staff of *Scientific American* magazine in New York. The December issue read, "Mr. Thomas A. Edison recently came into this office, placed a little machine on our desk, turned a crank, and the machine inquired as to our health, asked how we liked the phonograph, informed us that it was very well, and bid us a cordial good night." Newspapers and magazines reported this story. Interest in Edison's invention soared.

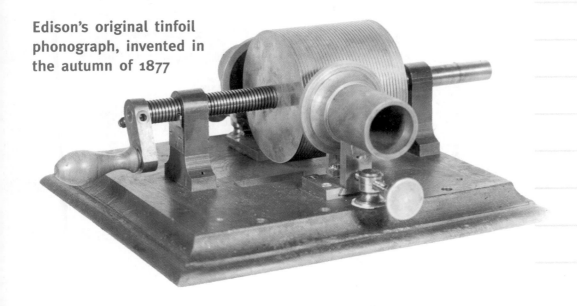

Edison's original tinfoil phonograph, invented in the autumn of 1877

6   Thomas Edison believed that everyone in America would want to have a phonograph machine. They would buy and listen to music in their homes. Unfortunately, the tinfoil did not last long, so the music could be played only a few times. Edison knew his phonograph needed improvement. At the time, he was also busy trying to invent a better lightbulb. While Edison worked on the lightbulb, other inventors such as Alexander Graham Bell and Charles Sumner Tainter improved Edison's phonograph. They replaced foil cylinders with cylinders made of wax. These made the sound much clearer.

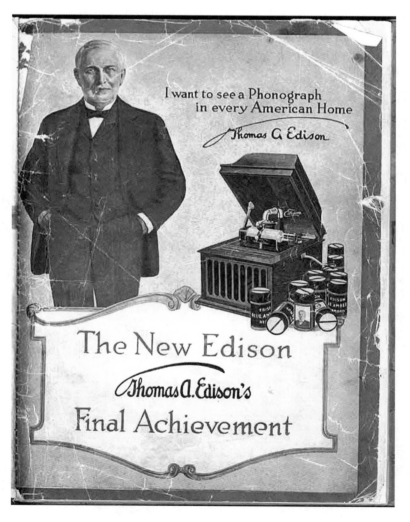

7   Once Edison finished his work on the lightbulb, he got back to improving the phonograph. First, he switched to wax cylinders. He used a thicker, harder wax. This made it possible to play the cylinder over 100 times. Then, Edison figured out a way to produce a lot of cylinders at one time. He developed a mold from a master cylinder. Then he used that one mold to produce more than 100 cylinders every day. Many records of the same music could now be sold. These cylinders were less expensive, so more people could afford to buy them.

The Gramophone

8   Edison and other inventors continued to improve the wax cylinder. In the late 1880s, Emile Berliner, another inventor, developed a new type of record. Instead of cylinders, he used flat discs to record sound. First, sound was recorded onto a wax disc. This disc was used to make a metal "master" copy of the recording. It was easier to make copies of it because of its flat design. Hundreds of copies could be made from the master. They were "stamped" out of a machine. The quality of the sound was much better on discs than on the wax cylinders.

9   The first discs were made of rubber. Later, these discs would be made of vinyl. People played their discs on a new device called a gramophone. The horn of the gramophone amplified the recorded sound. It was developed by Berliner and was similar to Edison's phonograph. People bought gramophones and phonographs to play all the recordings now available to them. Everyone could listen to the same marching band or singer perform the same music. It was the beginning of the recording business we know today.

Cool Stereo Sounds

10   Stereo recordings became widely available in the 1950s. With stereo, sounds were recorded on two separate tracks. One was meant to be heard in your right ear. The other would be heard in your left ear. This made recordings sound much richer and fuller than before.

Long-playing vinyl records were popular from the 1950s to the 1990s. Today, vinyl is making a comeback.

Compact discs replaced records and cassettes when music started being recorded with digital technology.

Cassettes on the Go

11   Compact cassettes became popular with music lovers in the 1970s. These cassettes recorded sounds on a long magnetic strip. Soon they outsold records. The 1979 introduction of the portable cassette player changed the music-listening experience even more. People could carry this small stereo system in a pocket. They wore headphones to listen to their favorite music wherever they went.

Compact Discs

12   The first compact disc, or CD, was released in 1982. A CD is a small plastic disc that stores music and other digital information. The CD player "reads" the information with laser light. The discs and players were expensive at first. But people saw their benefits. The discs were small and could hold more music than a record. Best of all, CDs produced almost perfect sound. It's no wonder that CDs soon began to replace records and cassettes.

A Digital World

13 Once personal computers and the Internet became commonplace, music could be stored on very small digital files. These files, such as MP3s, let people download music from the Internet quickly. People could now store hundreds of songs on a computer. No need to carry a physical disc or item anymore! But some people do not like the sound quality of these digital music files. They think CD recordings sound better.

14 The Apple iPod, released in 2001, became a popular personal media player. By the fall of 2010, almost 275 million iPods had been sold worldwide. After that time, sales began to drop. People started using smartphones as their personal media players.

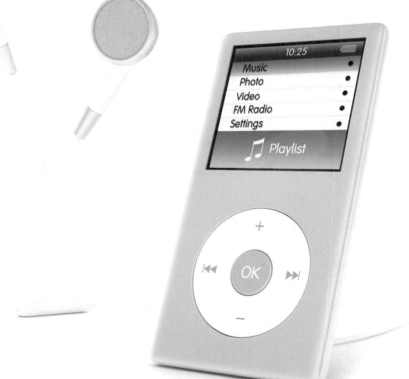

Today, people download music files from the Internet.

Playlists in the Cloud

15   Listening to music grew easier than ever. People could buy music from online stores in seconds. The music was never out of stock. People then stored the music in an invisible place on the Internet called "the cloud." And they did all this without leaving home.

16   Music-playing technology has changed a lot since Edison's first phonograph. Even so, the new devices do basically the same thing as the old one: they play your favorite music!

History of the Music

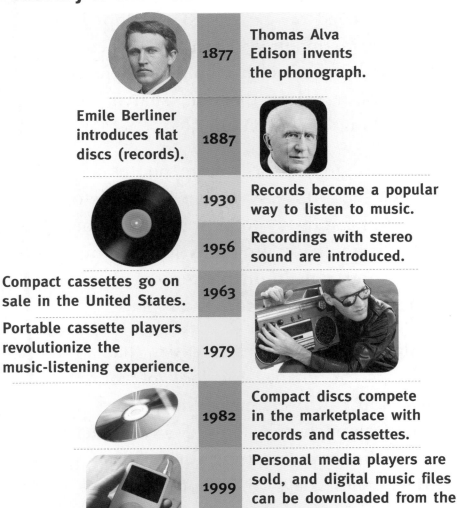

	1877	Thomas Alva Edison invents the phonograph.
Emile Berliner introduces flat discs (records).	1887	
	1930	Records become a popular way to listen to music.
	1956	Recordings with stereo sound are introduced.
Compact cassettes go on sale in the United States.	1963	
Portable cassette players revolutionize the music-listening experience.	1979	
	1982	Compact discs compete in the marketplace with records and cassettes.
	1999	Personal media players are sold, and digital music files can be downloaded from the Internet.

From Snapshots to Selfies

1   Many people today enjoy sharing pictures with friends. Some people like using old-style cameras to capture images. Others rely on their cell phones and digital devices.

2   People have been taking pictures for over a century. Early photographers carried glass plates and chemicals along with huge cameras. George Eastman introduced the smaller, simpler Kodak camera in 1888. This changed the way people thought about photography. Eastman made taking snapshots as easy as pressing a button!

3   People relied on experts to develop their film and print pictures. Then they taped or pasted their photos into albums or scrapbooks. Families gathered together and shared memories while looking at the pictures.

4   Today's digital devices store photos as computer files. It's easy to e-mail these to friends and family or to post them online. Some websites have programs for creating photo galleries. You can group photos together based on categories such as person or place.

5   Today, taking pictures is easier than ever. Some apps can change the look of your photos. You can even make the pictures look like old-fashioned snapshots. Many modern cameras also have a setting for "selfies," or self-portraits. These days, the photographer is often the subject!

BuildReflectWrite

Build Knowledge

Use a cause-and-effect chart to show how events in the development of sound recording led to new developments. One example is completed.

Cause	Effect
1. Edison's tinfoil cylinders could only be used a few times.	Creation of wax cylinders.
2.	
3.	

Reflect

What is the value of innovation?

Based on this week's texts, write down new ideas and questions you have about the essential question.

_____

_____

_____

_____

_____

_____

Writing to Sources

Opinion

Thomas Edison and Alexander Graham Bell were responsible for many brilliant inventions. Of all the inventions you read about in this unit, which do you think has been the most useful to people? Why? In a short essay, state your opinion and provide reasons to support it. Use facts and details from two of the unit selections you've read to explain your point of view.

Support for Collaborative Conversation

  ## Discussion Prompts

Share a new idea or opinion . . .

I think that _____.

I notice that _____.

My opinion is _____.

An important event was when _____.

Gain the floor . . .

I would like to add _____.

Excuse me for interrupting, but _____.

That made me think of _____.

Build on a peer's idea or opinion . . .

I also think that_____.

In addition, _____.

Another idea is _____.

Express agreement with a peer's idea . . .

I agree with [Name] because _____.

I agree that _____.

I think that is important because _____.

Respectfully express disagreement . . .

I disagree with [Name] because _____.

I understand your point of view, but I think _____.

Have you considered that _____?

Ask a clarifying question . . .

What did you mean when you said _____?

Are you saying that _____?

Can you explain what you mean by _____?

Clarify for others . . .

I meant that _____.

I am trying to say that _____.

Group Roles

Discussion Facilitator:
Your role is to guide the group discussion and make sure that everyone has the chance to participate.

Scribe:
Your job is to record the ideas and comments your group members share.

Timekeeper:
You will keep track of how much time has passed and help keep the discussion moving along.

Encourager:
Your role is to motivate and support your group members.

Making Meaning with Words

Word	My Definition	My Sentence
amplified (p. 26)		
commonplace (p. 28)		
device (p. 15)		
distant (p. 6)		
established (p. 5)		
innovative (p. 16)		
obtained (p. 19)		
revolutionary (p. 5)		
soared (p. 23)		
technology (p. 6)		

Lexile 590L–8

Build Knowledge Across
10 Topic Strands

 **Government and Citizenship**

Government for the People
WE ALL COUNT!

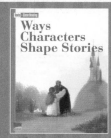 **Character**

Ways Characters Shape Stories

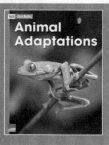 **Life Science**

Animal Adaptations

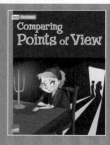 **Point of View**

Comparing Points of View

 **Technology and Society**

Advancements in Technology

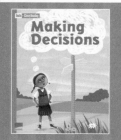 **Theme**

Making Decisions

 **History and Culture**

Communities Then and Now

 **Earth Science**

Weather and Climate

 **Economics**

Spending Time and Money

 **Physical Science**

FORCES AND Interactions

Grade 3 • Uni
ISBN 978-1-4900-
9 781490 091
T3-AAT-854